Encouraging Trade and Foreign Direct Investment in Ukraine

Keith Crane, F. Stephen Larrabee

Prepared for the
Institute of European and International Studies in Kyiv

RAND NATIONAL SECURITY RESEARCH DIVISION

The research described in this report was sponsored by the Institute of European and International Studies in Kyiv. It was conducted in the International Security and Defense Policy Center of the RAND National Security Research Division (NSRD). NSRD conducts research and analysis for the Office of the Secretary of Defense, the Joint Staff, the Unified Combatant Commands, the defense agencies, the Department of the Navy, the Marine Corps, the U.S. Coast Guard, the U.S. Intelligence Community, allied foreign governments, and U.S. and foreign foundations.

Library of Congress Cataloging-in-Publication Data is available for this publication.

ISBN 978-0-8330-4216-3

Cover Design by Stephen Bloodsworth

Published 2007 by the RAND Corporation
1776 Main Street, P.O. Box 2138, Santa Monica, CA 90407-2138
1200 South Hayes Street, Arlington, VA 22202-5050
4570 Fifth Avenue, Suite 600, Pittsburgh, PA 15213-2665
RAND URL: http://www.rand.org/
To order RAND documents or to obtain additional information, contact
Distribution Services: Telephone: (310) 451-7002;
Fax: (310) 451-6915; Email: order@rand.org

Preface

This monograph presents an analysis of the current environment for foreign trade and investment in Ukraine and a set of policy proposals that would serve to expand foreign trade and attract more foreign direct investment in Ukraine, especially with respect to the United States.

The project was sponsored by the Institute of European and International Studies in Kyiv. It was conducted within the International Security and Defense Policy Center of the RAND Corporation's National Security Research Division (NSRD). NSRD conducts research and analysis for the Office of the Secretary of Defense, the Joint Staff, the Unified Combatant Commands, the defense agencies, the Department of the Navy, the Marine Corps, the U.S. Coast Guard, the U.S. Intelligence Community, allied foreign governments, and U.S. and foreign foundations.

For more information on RAND's International Security and Defense Policy Center, contact the Director, James Dobbins. He can be reached by email at dobbins@rand.org; by phone at 703-413-1100, extension 5134; or by mail at the RAND Corporation, 1200 South Hayes Street, Arlington, VA 22202-5050. More information about RAND is available at www.rand.org.

Contents

Figures

Summary

Ukrainian governments have found it singularly difficult to liberalize trade and improve the climate for foreign direct investment (FDI), ostensibly two of Ukraine's economic policy priorities. Trade and FDI have greatly contributed to economic growth and increases in standards of living throughout the world, especially in Central Europe. However, in contrast to Central Europe, Ukraine has been slow to open its borders to trade and has had difficulty attracting sizable inflows of FDI. As a result, Ukraine has suffered economically: Its standards of living are currently far below those in Central Europe, Russia, and Kazakhstan.

Barriers to Trade and Foreign Direct Investment in Ukraine

Corruption

Corruption, petty and grand, constitutes the single greatest barrier to expanding trade and investment in Ukraine. Grand corruption involves high-level officials with discretionary authority over government policy, the sale of government assets, or large government contracts. Petty corruption involves lower-level officials who make decisions about enforcing (or not enforcing) regulations.

Foreign businesses complain most vociferously about Ukrainian regulatory and legal hurdles designed to elicit bribes. As in most countries afflicted by corruption, Ukrainian government employees, in hopes of eliciting bribes, deliberately design licensing and registration procedures to be so complex that they may credibly threaten to halt or slow trade or a foreign investment. As a consequence, the time and expense of obtaining the requisite permits and licenses to trade or to set up and open a business add substantially to costs, reducing both trade and investment. Rigged privatizations also impede foreign investment. Ukraine's contradictory laws and corrupt judges make it difficult for businesses to enforce contracts, which also discourages investment.

Barriers to Trade

The most immediate problem facing Ukraine is that it is not yet a member of the World Trade Organization (WTO) despite support for this step from all major political parties. Because Ukraine is not a member of the WTO, Ukrainian firms face discriminatory treatment in most of their export markets. Exporters and importers in Ukraine confront arbitrary changes in domestic policies because the Ukrainian government is unconstrained by treaty obligations.

The most severe impediment to exports in Ukraine is the corruption embedded in the system for providing rebates to exporters for value-added tax (VAT). Government employees encourage companies seeking VAT refunds to hire local law or consulting firms that charge a "fee" of 25 to 30 percent of the refund to expedite reimbursements. Companies that hire these firms have their VAT reimbursed promptly; companies that do not, wait three to 18 months for reimbursement. Smaller companies sometimes receive no refunds at all.

The greatest barrier for importers is Ukraine's complex, corrupt system of certifying imports. The accepted international practice is for importing countries to recognize products certified by accredited bodies in partner states with internationally recognized accreditation procedures as acceptable. In Ukraine, all products subject to mandatory certification—which constitute a very long list—have to be recertified, substantially increasing importers' costs.

Nothing has undermined Ukraine's reputation as a responsible trading partner more than the embargoes imposed on grain exports in 2006 and 2007. These embargoes were instigated by Ukrainian commercial interests tied to the government that hoped to obtain export quotas and resell them to legitimate grain exporters, pocketing substantial sums in the process. This policy caused legitimate grain exporters to lose upwards of $200 million. Additionally, it will have a lasting, depressing effect on the incomes of Ukrainian farmers given that international grain trading companies now shun the Ukrainian market because of the risks of export embargoes and quotas.

Barriers to Foreign Direct Investment

Potential investors have great difficulty obtaining satisfactory sites in Ukraine. Potential investors cannot obtain the land they need to build distribution centers and factories. Retailers and restaurateurs complain that municipal governments sell or lease all the best commercial sites to favored individuals. Problems in obtaining titles, construction permits, and operating permits add to costs and complexity.

A number of provisions in the 2004 Commercial (or Economic) Code contradict existing provisions in the more market-oriented, Civil Code. Businesses find that activities mandated by one of these codes sometimes violate provisions of the other. Some Ukrainian businesses exploit these legal discrepancies by selecting the laws they find preferable for their current operations. If disputes arise, they choose courts that favor their choice of applicable laws or judges who are willing to be bribed to do so.

Because of deficiencies in the laws pertaining to joint stock companies, shareholders lack key rights of ownership. Majority shareholders can use the legal system and a friendly court to issue new shares and steal assets. Minority shareholders ("raiders") have used current laws to deprive majority shareholders of their rights and, in a few instances, control of their company.

In contrast to the governments of Central Europe, Ukrainian governments have not extensively used privatization to attract foreign capital and business expertise. With the exception of a very few transparent sales of major assets, privatization has resulted in formerly state-owned enterprises being acquired by Ukrainian businessmen or foreign companies controlled by Ukrainians. In most instances, Ukrainian businessmen have effectively excluded foreign investors by usurping the privatization process.

Current laws and policies, ostensibly designed to make it possible for foreigners to invest in Ukraine's energy sector, effectively discourage most potential investors. Those companies that have invested in Ukraine's energy sector have experienced difficulties with Ukrainian regulators. Some decisions have been in violation of the law or based on extraordinarily narrow interpretations of regulations.

Recommendations for Improving the Climate for Trade and Foreign Direct Investment in Ukraine

The Ukrainian government should adopt a two-pronged strategy to remove the worst of these impediments to trade and investment. First, the government should focus on making a few highly visible policy changes that promise results within 100 days. Second, the government should set in motion changes in Ukraine's institutions that will, with time, reduce corruption and other impediments to trade and investment. Several recommendations whose adoption would reduce the most egregious barriers to trade and FDI are provided below. We have classified them according to whether they are expected to bring results within 100 days or over a longer period.

Corruption

Within the next 100 days, the Ukrainian government should do the following to reduce opportunities for government employees to manipulate the regulatory system in order to solicit bribes:

- Set up a network of regional boards to which businesses and citizens can appeal administrative decisions. The boards should be composed of civil servants, businessmen, and citizens, and should have the authority to stay decisions taken by lower-level civil servants until they can be reviewed by higher-level administrators or administrative courts. All board meetings should be open to the public.
- Give Inspector Generals the authority to immediately put government employees facing credible accusations of soliciting bribes on administrative leave and to then quickly bring cases to court for resolution.

- Hold supervisors responsible for the behavior of their employees, and reprimand or dismiss supervisors whose employees have been convicted of corruption.

Fostering Trade

Joining the WTO is the most important near-term step that the Ukrainian government can take to spur trade. If bilateral negotiations fail to resolve issues with current WTO members that threaten to block Ukraine's entry, the Ukrainian government should turn to the secretariat of the WTO, the U.S. government, or the European Commission for assistance in resolving these issues.

The Ukrainian government will need to maintain an interministerial working group with the clout to prevent laws or regulations being made that violate Ukraine's agreements with the WTO. *The Ukrainian government should give the Department on Cooperation with the WTO full authority to ensure that Ukrainian legislation and regulations remain in compliance with the WTO.*

The Ukrainian government should promptly reimburse exporters for VAT payments. Regulations should be issued stipulating that VAT reimbursement requests be processed in accordance with the law (that is, within 60 days). Supervisors should be penalized if the regulations are not followed.

Ukraine should immediately accept all products that conform to European Union (EU) standards. Once a product is certified by the EU, no further certification should be necessary in Ukraine.

The Ukrainian government should immediately eliminate all remaining embargoes on grains. It should pass legislation conforming to WTO practices that strictly defines when export quotas on agricultural products may be imposed and how they will be allocated.

Attracting Foreign Direct Investment

The Ukrainian government should set legal limits on the ability of government employees to impede the establishment of businesses in Ukraine. The government should

- Set fixed deadlines for action on permits.

- Set a yearly limit on the number of inspections to which a business will be subject.
- Ensure that initiatives for one-stop registrations and permits are operating by January 1, 2008.

The Ukrainian government should ensure that its decision to repeal the ban on agricultural land sales goes into effect on January 1, 2008.

The Ukrainian government should immediately abolish the Commercial Code and appoint a task force to revise the Civil Code. The task force should be composed of representatives from the judiciary, government agencies, the legal profession, businesses, and consumer groups. It should provide draft legislation or regulations to fix laws affecting Ukrainian businesses that are contradictory, poorly written, or lacking. It should also appoint a small team of senior government officials to spearhead efforts to make the necessary legislative changes.

The Ukrainian government should replace its current privatization strategy with a new one that is geared toward rapid, transparent privatization of almost all the commercial assets it still owns. The government should create a revised list of companies to be privatized and an accelerated time schedule for privatization. It should also establish clear procedures for issuing tenders for trade sales, permit all interested parties to bid, and publish the terms of all bids and the winning bid. The highest bid should win.

To ensure adequate, competitive supplies of energy, the Ukrainian government should actively seek FDI in the energy sector. To encourage foreign investment in domestic production of oil and gas, the government should lengthen the current five-year production-sharing agreements to ten to 20 years, periods customary elsewhere in the world. In addition, the government should increase the wholesale prices of Ukrainian natural gas to those of imported gas. It should also encourage foreign investors to participate in the construction and ownership of new gas and oil transit pipelines.

Acknowledgments

This report benefited greatly from the insights and suggestions of numerous investors, managers, government officials, and analysts both in and outside Ukraine. We would like to express our deep appreciation for the assistance of the following individuals: Dr. Irina Akimova, Bureau of Economic and Social Technologies; Dr. Anders Aslund, Peterson Institute of International Economics; Edward Chow, Center for Strategic and International Studies; Dr. Elisabetta Falcetti, European Bank for Reconstruction and Development; Alexander Gorodetsky, Interpipe Corporation; Mark Iwashko, Western NIS Enterprise Fund; Douglas Kramer, Economic Counselor, U.S. Embassy in Ukraine; Gary Litman, Vice President, Europe and Eurasia, U.S. Chamber of Commerce; Lidiya Melnyk, Deputy Director, Ministry of Economy of Ukraine; Jock Mendoza-Wilson, System Capital Management; former U.S. Ambassador to Ukraine William Miller; Lauri Molnar, Office of the United States Trade Representative; Pavel Moyseychenko, Ministry of Economy of Ukraine; Olga Oliker, RAND Corporation; Ambassador Steven Pifer, Center for Strategic and International Studies; Andrea Raffaseder, Siemens Ukraine; Andreas Rickmers, Cargill; Ihor Shevliakov, International Centre for Policy Studies; Dr. Farooq Siddiqui, International Steel and Tube Industries; Ambassador William Taylor, U.S. Embassy in Ukraine; Serheii Teriokhin, member of the Verkovna Rada; Morgan Williams, Sigma-Bleyzer; Ihor Petrovich Zahlada, Director, Ukrainian Center for Promotion of Foreign Investment; Svetlana Petrivna Zaitseva, Ministry of Economy of Ukraine; and Jorge Zukoski, American Chamber of Commerce in Ukraine.

CHAPTER ONE

Introduction

Successive Ukrainian governments have found it singularly difficult to pass legislation needed to pursue what are ostensibly economic policy priorities. Passing legislation and implementing policies to liberalize trade and improve the climate for foreign direct investment (FDI) have been especially difficult. The purpose of this study was to identify major barriers to trade and deficiencies in the current environment for FDI in Ukraine and to develop concrete policy recommendations for removing these barriers and improving the climate for FDI.

In our view, the Ukrainian government would be better served by adopting and successfully implementing a few key policies than by trying to simultaneously address the myriad weaknesses and deficiencies that afflict its current economic policy. Our study sought to provide politically persuasive arguments for the adoption of such policies. Additionally, in focusing on barriers to trade and the environment for FDI in general, we chose to pay particular attention to how they affect economic relations between Ukraine and the United States.

There has been no dearth of studies on Ukraine's trade policies and FDI climate. The Office of the United States Trade Representative provides detailed annual assessments of barriers to trade with Ukraine.[1] The European Business Association has published four (soon to be five) reports itemizing barriers to business operations and investment in Ukraine.[2] The Blue Ribbon Commission has provided numer-

[1] Office of the United States Trade Representative, 2007.

[2] European Business Association, *Barriers to Investment in Ukraine*, various editions.

ous recommendations on economic policy, including policy changes that would stimulate foreign trade and serve to attract more FDI.[3]

Our study drew on this past work while focusing on policy changes and administrative reforms that would have the highest payoff in terms of improving the environment for trade and FDI. We also outlined political strategies that would make it easier to adopt these policy changes.

Missed Opportunities

Why Foster Foreign Trade or Seek Foreign Direct Investment?

Trade and FDI have contributed heavily to economic growth and increases in standards of living throughout the world, especially in countries in Central Europe and East Asia. Trade has provided better-quality, lower-cost products that have dramatically improved the quality of life of citizens of these countries. Local businesses have thrived by increasing exports to new markets. Competitive pressures from imports have raised local standards, spurring improvements in quality and productivity at home that have led to higher incomes for local citizens.

The benefits of trade liberalization are especially great in smaller economies, which lack the full array of industries needed to competitively produce a wide assortment of products. Smaller economies often have an advantage in a few key industries that need export markets to grow. Although Ukraine is a fairly large European country in terms of population and geography, its economy is small. In 2006, Ukraine's gross domestic product (GDP) was $103 billion, a little less than Hungary's GDP of $112 billion. Thus, the gains for Ukraine from expanding trade would be large.

FDI has been a major factor driving rapid economic growth in Central and Southeastern Europe and East Asia over the last decade and a half. In the transition economies of Central and Southeastern Europe, it has provided badly needed capital to construct new plants and modernize older ones. Equally important, foreign owners have

---

3 Blue Ribbon Commission for Ukraine, 2005.

introduced new technologies, better business practices, and improvements in marketing and management. And these benefits have not been confined solely to the operations of foreign-owned plants. Many of the new entrepreneurs in Central and Southeastern Europe learned better management practices and established ties with foreign customers while working for subsidiaries of foreign companies. They then used their knowledge and ties to branch out on their own, creating new businesses, increasing productivity, and accelerating economic growth.

Despite its economic benefits, FDI is often politically sensitive. Sales of large politically salient plants trigger political concerns about loss of national control over industries that impinge on daily life (such as electric power) or that affect national security (such as defense industries or natural gas pipelines). Although no political party in Central Europe has lost power because it permitted FDI, citizens often voice concern about the sale of prominent national corporations to foreign investors. Political opponents of sitting governments frequently charge that the national patrimony has been sold to foreign investors for less than it is worth. Sales of land and mineral deposits are especially contentious. Domestic business groups complain about "unfair" competition from foreign firms. When foreign companies hold large stakes in the local economy, citizens fear foreign interference in domestic politics.

These political concerns cannot be ignored, but special interests should not be permitted to exploit them to impede competition from imports or derail FDI. In most instances, arguments against reduced barriers to trade or improving the climate for FDI are driven by the parochial interests of cosseted domestic business groups or bureaucracies that manipulate current regulations to charge higher prices or demand bribes.

Breaking down the barriers to expanded trade and foreign investment is no easy task. By joining the World Trade Organization (WTO), signing free trade agreements with the European Union (EU), and ultimately becoming members of the EU, the Central European states have successfully eliminated many of the barriers. The result has been an unprecedented increase in living standards and wealth. Estonia, which is one of the countries that have gone the furthest in liberalizing their economies, has seen per capita income rise 3.6 times over the course of a decade—from $3,180 in 1996 to $11,500 in 2006. All the Central European states have registered large increases in per capita income. In contrast, despite several years of solid growth, Ukraine's per capita GDP was $2,220 in 2006. If Ukraine is to enjoy the higher standards of living that the Baltic and Central European states have attained, it will have to aggressively break down current barriers to both trade and FDI.

Ukraine Has Been Slow to Foster Trade or Seek Foreign Direct Investment

In contrast to the governments of Central and Southeastern Europe, Ukrainian governments have been slow to open the country's borders to trade. Ukrainian businesses find it difficult to import key components because they face a barrier of certification requirements, tariffs, and requests for bribes. The government penalizes exporters by levying export taxes, which often fall most heavily on some of Ukraine's poorest citizens. For example, Ukrainian farmers, who tend to fall into the lowest income groups, are subject to a 16 percent tax on exports of sunflower seeds, which sharply cuts their income from this crop. The government also rebates value-added tax (VAT) payments to exporters slowly, if at all, which penalizes exporters.

Only recently has Ukraine succeeded in attracting sizable inflows of FDI. Prior to 2003, FDI never exceeded $800 million per year, a dismal performance for a country of Ukraine's size. Potential investors have been put off by difficulties in procuring business licenses, permission for expatriate staff to work in Ukraine, and land for commercial or industrial premises. State-owned enterprises have been sold to friends of the regime, not the highest bidders. Tax laws have been complicated and contradictory while tax authorities have been quick to exact large penalties for small mistakes or infractions.

The governments installed following the Orange Revolution were expected to adopt policies that would foster trade and FDI. In 2005, U.S. businessmen and investors gave Ukraine a second look when it appeared that its accession to the WTO was imminent and that the revolution would be followed by concerted attempts to reduce bureaucratic obstacles to trade and investment. The Orange Coalition's failure to form a durable government following the 2006 parliamentary elections and the decision by President Viktor Yushchenko to make Viktor Yanukovych prime minister in August 2006 left markets and investors bewildered about the likely future course of economic policy.

The current Ukrainian government has sent mixed signals to investors and businessmen. On the one hand, Prime Minister Yanukovych has made significant efforts to declare Ukraine "open for business." On the other hand, differentiated reimbursements for VAT, the abrupt adoption of export quotas for grain, reports of discriminatory practices by the Yanukovych cabinet, and the reconstitution of special economic zones suggest that the government is practicing "business as usual." Frustration and confusion abound among Western economic policymakers, businessmen, and investors while favored corporate interests prosper.

If the Ukrainian economy is to thrive, the government must develop coherent, effective policies to foster trade and attract FDI. Currently, flows of both trade and FDI are far below what they should be in light of Ukraine's dynamic, well-educated population, developed industry, and natural resources. Poorly designed government policies are hampering Ukraine's development. A new set of effective policies is needed.

Research Approach

Research for our study proceeded along three lines. We first gathered available statistical information on trade and FDI flows for Ukraine. Data of interest were taken from Ukraine's balance of payments and foreign investment position, as well as from data on the value of FDI by country of origin. These statistics were obtained from the State Statistics Committee of Ukraine and the National Bank of Ukraine.

Second, we reviewed past sets of recommendations, most notably the reports of the European Business Association and the Blue Ribbon Commission, on barriers to investment in Ukraine. We used these reports not only as a source of ideas, but also as a basis for our evaluation of why past recommendations have not been adopted or implemented. The reports helped ground our recommendations on what steps would be the most important for fostering trade and foreign direct investment in Ukraine and which policy measures would be most likely to be implemented.

Third, we conducted interviews with U.S. and other foreign investors and business groups in both the United States and Ukraine to determine what contributes to and detracts from trading with and investing in Ukraine. Data from these interviews constitute the heart of this report. We asked how their decisions on trade and investment in Ukraine were influenced by barriers to trade and investment, macroeconomic policies, and political instability. In Ukraine, we interviewed both foreign and Ukrainian business leaders, business groups, members of the financial and research communities, employees of international lending institutions, and Ukrainian government officials and leaders. We targeted individuals who had firsthand knowledge of investment practices and foreign investments within Ukraine. More than two dozen discussions were held. Our interlocutors were generous with their time and insights, sharing their experiences and observations from day-to-day activities in the business community and with the governments of Ukraine.

Organization of This Monograph

Following this introduction, we assess the current status of trade and FDI in Ukraine. We evaluate recent trends in Ukrainian trade, including trends in trade with the United States. We then estimate the stock of FDI and the FDI inflows into Ukraine, comparing relative sizes and favored sectors.

In Chapter Three, we evaluate barriers to trade and FDI in Ukraine, with an emphasis on barriers affecting the United States. We highlight those barriers that have served most to constrain this trade and FDI.

Chapter Four provides recommendations on policy changes that would reduce barriers to trade and attract more FDI. These concrete recommendations are accompanied by a discussion of implementation strategies and ways to ensure that the recommendations operate as intended.

CHAPTER TWO

Foreign Trade, Foreign Direct Investment, and the Ukrainian Economy

Ukrainian Economic Growth: The Record

Of all the former Soviet republics, Ukraine suffered the longest and one of the deepest declines in economic activity. Its transition recession lasted from 1989 until 2000, 11 years (Figure 2.1). According to official statistics, Ukraine's GDP by 1999 was just 38.5 percent of its 1989 level. Since 1999, the economy has grown rapidly; growth in GDP has averaged 7.3 percent per year. Nonetheless, Ukraine's GDP in 2006 was still only two-thirds of its peak.

The factors that have driven recovery in Ukraine have been more akin to those in Russia than to those in the Central European states. A prime driver has been rapid growth in output from plants constructed during the Soviet era, primarily in the export industries of ferrous and non-ferrous metals, machine building, and chemicals. Increases in output from the large privately owned industrial conglomerates that were created from formerly state-owned enterprises have contributed heavily to a doubling of Ukraine's industrial output since 1998.

As is true for Russia and other former Soviet republics, Ukraine owes its recovery more to construction, telecommunications (especially cellular telephones), finance, and business and personal services than to manufacturing. Because the service sector was neglected during Soviet times, output in these sectors has soared. Increases in output from small privately owned firms have also been an important driver of economic growth. New plants in the nascent private sector have resulted

Figure 2.1
Ukraine's GDP, 1989–2007

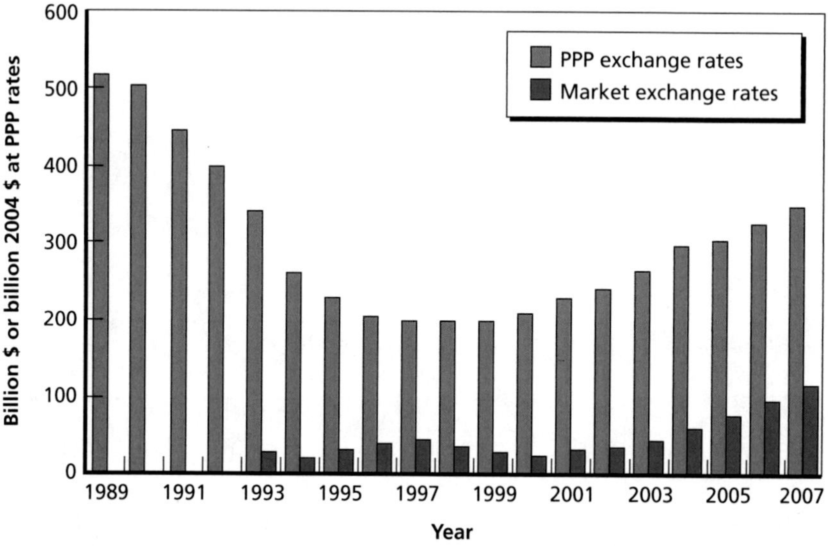

SOURCE: State Statistics Committee of Ukraine, "National Accounts," years shown.
RAND *MG673-2.1*

in increased output from the food processing, textiles, and clothing branches. Increases in output from agriculture, government services, and coal mining have lagged the overall rate of growth in GDP.

Ukraine's growth record is probably even better than it appears to be. The State Statistics Committee of Ukraine reported that GDP rose just 2.7 percent in 2005, down sharply from the increase of 12.1 percent recorded in 2004. Most of the slowdown in growth stemmed from declines in value added from construction and from wholesale and retail trade. However, retail sales boomed in 2005, up 23 percent in real terms, and yet value added from wholesale and retail trade reportedly fell 8.3 percent. This discrepancy is highly suspect. One respected source has argued that elimination of Special Economic Zones in that year, which had been a source of wide-scale tax evasion on imported goods, skewed statistics on value added in trade for 2005.[1] If value

1 PlanEcon, 2006, p. 52.

added in trade had been more accurately measured, Ukrainian GDP growth for 2005 would have been at least 5 percent, and probably substantially more.

Despite recent rapid growth, Ukraine is poorer than its neighbors. While East Asia and Central Europe were enjoying growth during the 1990s, Ukraine's decline in output drove its 1999 per capita GDP to just 40.3 percent of its 1989 level. The decline in per capita GDP was a little less than the overall decline in output because Ukraine's population fell 4.7 percent over this period, as life expectancy remained low and many Ukrainians emigrated to Central and Western Europe and Russia in search of better-paying jobs. By 2006, per capita GDP ran $2,200, putting Ukraine among the middle-income developing countries. Using purchasing power parity (PPP) exchange rates, per capita GDP was still only $7,100 in 2006.

Per capita GDP is far lower in Ukraine than in Russia, Kazakhstan, and the three Baltic states (Figure 2.2). Ukraine's per capita GDP is a fifth of Estonia's and a third of Russia's at market exchange rates. The more favorable comparison, that based on PPP exchange rates, still shows that Ukraine's per capita GDP is half that of the Baltic states and two-thirds that of Russia. Wages are substantially lower than in these countries, as well. In May 2007, monthly wages ran $238 in Ukraine compared with $472 in Russia.

Using the World Bank's $2-a-day definition of poverty, 4.9 percent of Ukrainians were poor in 2005. Of the European countries, virtually only Moldova has citizens who, like these Ukrainians, live on less than $2 a day. Ukraine scores better in international comparisons using local measures of deprivation: In 2003, 19 percent of its population was classified as poor, which is smaller than the shares classified as poor in Poland, Russia, and Lithuania.[2] Since the beginning of the recovery, poverty has declined more rapidly in Ukraine than in a number of other transition economies, including Poland and Russia.

Why has Ukraine been so slow to enjoy the benefits of transition? In comparison with most of the other transition countries, including

---

2 World Bank, 2005, p. vii.

Figure 2.2
Per Capita GDP for Selected Former Soviet Republics, 2006

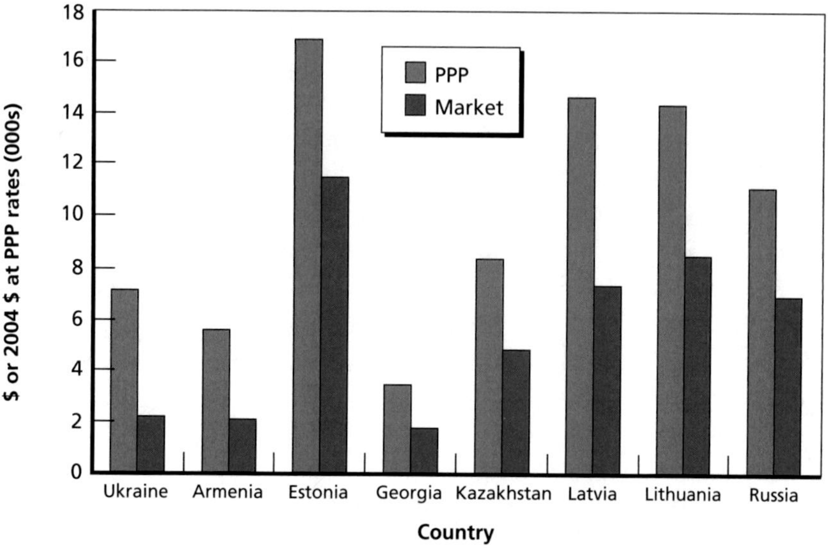

SOURCE: Eurostat, "National Accounts: Gross Domestic Product," 2006; State Statistics Committee of Ukraine, "National Accounts," 2006; IMF, International Financial Statistics, 2007.
RAND *MG673-2.2*

Russia, Ukraine's new private-sector economic activities were slow to emerge. As late as 2002, Ukraine had only 18.5 incorporated businesses per 1,000 population, whereas Russia's number was more than a third higher. Barriers to entry imposed by corrupt government officials and bureaucrats, the slow pace of privatization, and the initial absence of dynamic, profitable export industries retarded recovery.

Because Ukraine's investment climate has been perceived as hostile, the country has failed to enjoy the benefits from large inflows of FDI. Because of low levels of FDI, output from subsidiaries of multinational firms has contributed little to Ukraine's recovery, in contrast to the positive impact that FDI has had on economic growth in Central Europe.

Ukraine's Foreign Trade

Evolution and Principal Trading Partners

Despite many government-imposed barriers to exports, Ukrainian businessmen have begun to export aggressively. As can be seen in Figure 2.3, Ukrainian exports grew slowly in the mid-1990s and declined between 1997 and 1999 (as Russian demand fell sharply following the crash of the ruble). But since then, they have surged, more than tripling by 2006.

Exports have played a key role in Ukraine's recovery. Rising productivity and cost reductions have made Ukrainian heavy industry a formidable exporter. Ukraine has also benefited from increases in world market prices. A surge in demand for steel from China, Russia, and other rapidly growing economies boosted this decade's demand for metals and chemicals, sparking price increases and providing an additional impetus to exports.

Figure 2.3
Ukraine's Exports, 1994–2006

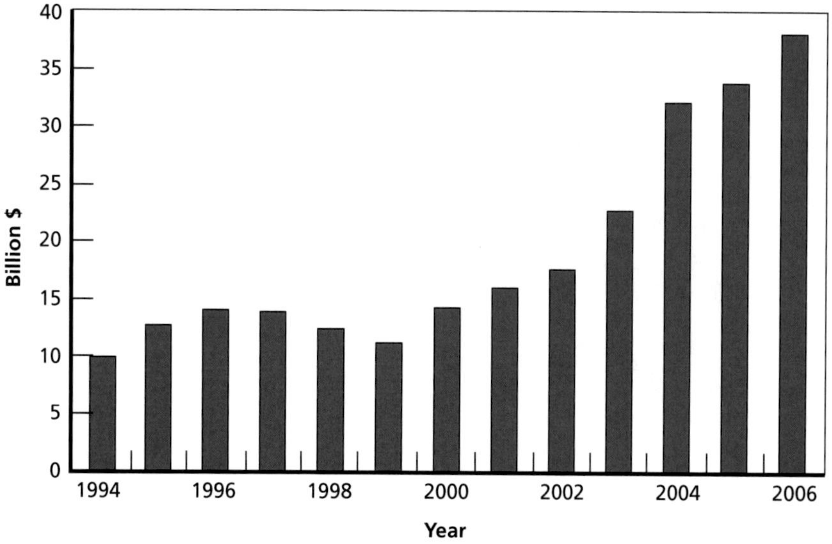

SOURCE: State Statistics Committee of Ukraine, "National Accounts," years shown.
RAND *MG673-2.3*

Exports have also risen rapidly because Ukrainian exporters have found new markets. The EU is now Ukraine's largest export market, having displaced Russia in 1998 (Figure 2.4). But growth in exports to Asia, especially China, has outpaced growth in exports to the EU since 2002. Within the EU, the larger EU economies of Italy and Germany rank among Ukraine's top three export markets. But a number of Ukraine's former Communist neighbors rank among Ukraine's top ten EU markets: Poland, Hungary, Romania, Bulgaria, and Slovakia, in order of importance. Ukraine's exports to each of these countries exceed its exports to either France or the United Kingdom. Outside of the EU, Russia, Belarus, and China loom large.

Ukraine's imports are even more concentrated by region than its exports are. Over four-fifths of Ukraine's imports come from other countries in the Commonwealth of Independent States (CIS) or from Europe, primarily the EU (Figure 2.5). In 2006, the EU edged out Russia as Ukraine's primary source of imports. Russia and Turkmen-

Figure 2.4
Ukraine's Exports, by Region and Country, 2006

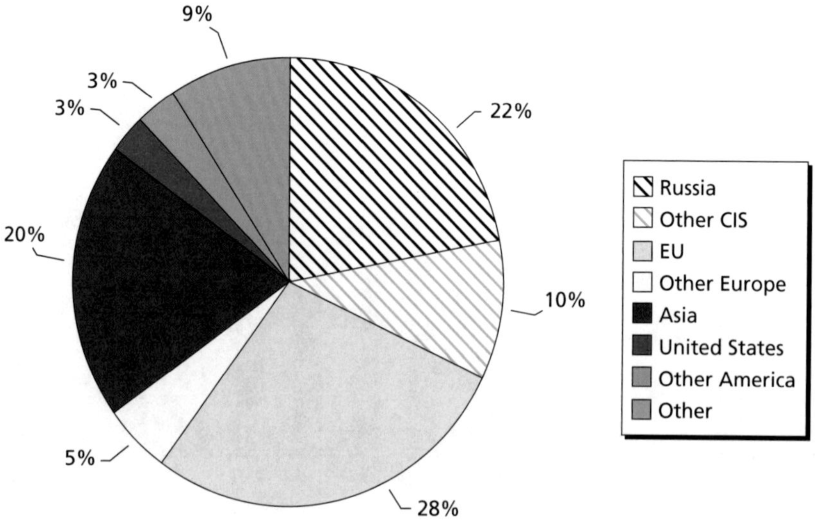

SOURCE: State Statistics Committee of Ukraine, "National Accounts," 2006.
RAND *MG673-2.4*

Figure 2.5
Ukraine's Imports, by Region and Country, 2006

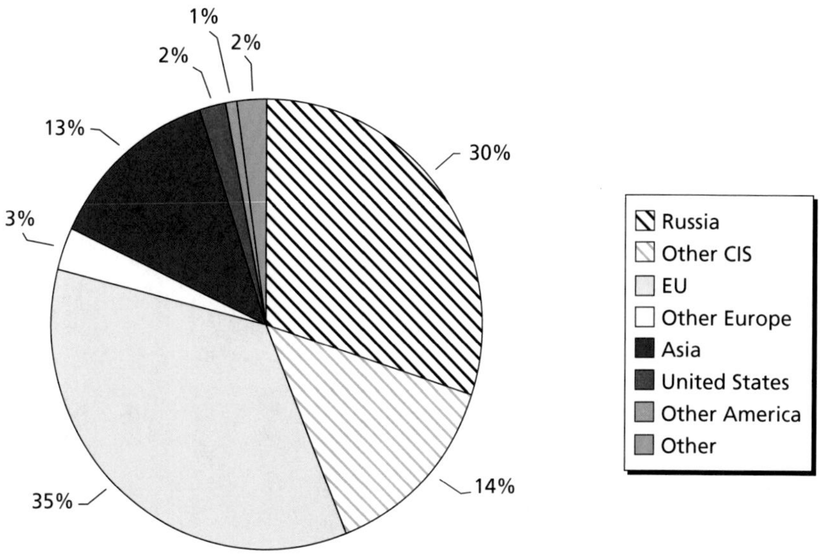

SOURCE: State Statistics Committee of Ukraine, "National Accounts," 2006.
RAND *MG673-2.5*

istan are virtually the sole sources of Ukraine's imports of energy. Ukraine imports a number of other commodities from Russia, such as chemicals, metals, and wood. Machinery and consumer goods play a more important role in imports from the EU and Asia.

Trade with the United States

Figure 2.6 shows Ukraine's trade with the United States. At $1.2 billion, the United States is Ukraine's eighth largest export market, just behind Belarus. Exports to the United States have fluctuated in recent years, although the general trend has been upward. Since 2000, exports to the EU and Russia, Ukraine's two largest export markets, have grown more rapidly than exports to the United States, in both relative and absolute terms. Ukraine's exports to the United States are heavily concentrated in metals and inorganic chemicals; these two categories accounted for four-fifths of the total in 2006. Transport costs,

Figure 2.6
Ukraine's Trade with the United States, 1996–2006

SOURCE: State Statistics Committee of Ukraine, "National Accounts," 1996–2006.
RAND *MG673-2.6*

barriers to trade, lack of favorable bilateral trade relations, and limited knowledge of the U.S. market have limited Ukrainian exports of other items to the United States.

Ukraine's imports from the United States have grown steadily since their nadir in 1998. The items imported are more widely dispersed across commodity categories than are the exports to the United States. The two most important imports, special industrial machinery and motor vehicles, account for just a quarter of imports from the United States, which stands in contrast to the very concentrated nature of Ukraine's exports.

Foreign Direct Investment in Ukraine

After a slow start, Ukraine has begun to enjoy appreciable inflows of foreign investment, especially since 2003 (Figure 2.7). Nonetheless,

Figure 2.7
Cumulative Foreign Direct Investment in Ukraine and Hungary

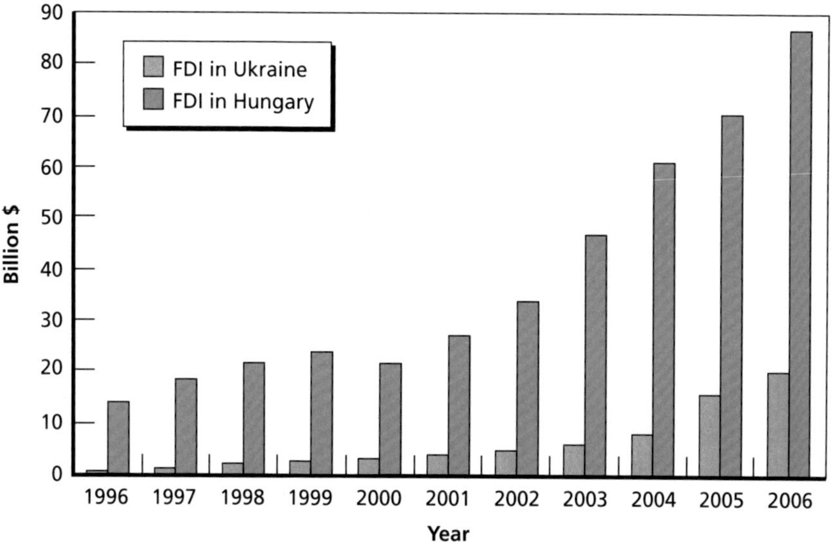

SOURCE: State Statistics Committee of Ukraine, "National Accounts," 1996–2006; International Monetary Fund, 2007.
RAND *MG673-2.7*

Ukraine's cumulative FDI has remained modest, reaching $21.2 billion at the end of 2006, compared with $88 billion for Hungary, an economy of comparable size. Annual inflows only surpassed $1 billion for the first time in 2003. Ukraine scores even more poorly on a per capita basis. In 2006, Ukraine's cumulative per capita FDI was $456, compared with Hungary's $8,700 and Russia's $1,293.

Germany is the largest single investor in Ukraine. In 2005, Germany more than doubled its investment in Ukraine when the Mittal Group used its German subsidiary to purchase Krivoryzhstal, Ukraine's largest steel complex. Cyprus ranks second (Figure 2.8); its investment is a combination of both Russian and Ukrainian investments. Russians find it easier to invest in Ukraine from Cyprus than from their home country; wealthy Ukrainians, like their Russian counterparts, park their money abroad and then repatriate it to purchase attractive assets in Ukraine as they become available. The figures for Russia,

Figure 2.8
Cumulative Foreign Direct Investment in Ukraine, by Country of Origin, 2006

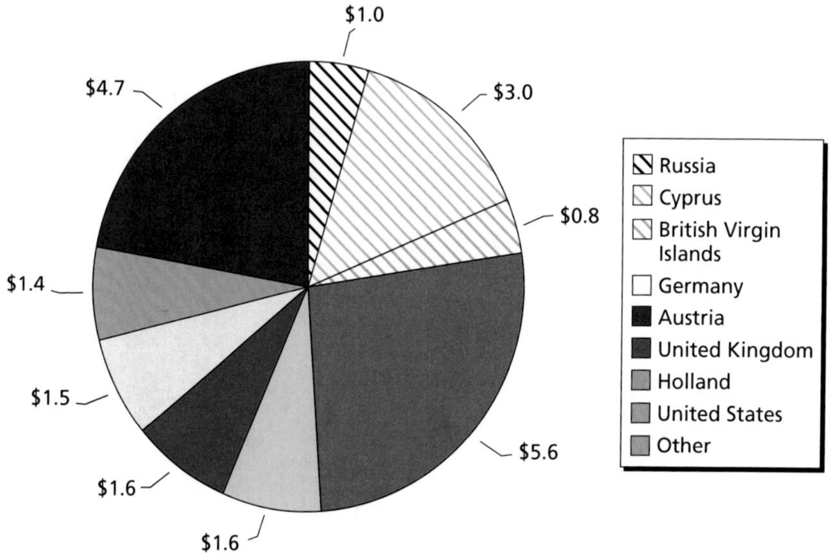

SOURCE: State Statistics Committee of Ukraine, "National Accounts," 2006.
RAND *MG673-2.8*

Cyprus, and the British Virgin Islands (another place to park cash that is popular with Russian and Ukrainian investors) run a cumulative 23 percent of total FDI in Ukraine. Austria, the United Kingdom, the Netherlands, and the United States have all made sizable investments in Ukraine.

Because of the purchase of Krivoryzhstal, the steel industry has attracted more capital than any other sector in Ukraine. However, banking is the most vibrant sector. Since 2006, banking has attracted the most substantial investment. Over a fifth of banking capital in Ukraine is now owned by foreign investors. Agriculture—most notably sunflower-seed processing, agricultural inputs, and grain trading—has also attracted large sums going back to the 1990s. In addition, foreign investors have put money into the automotive industry, consumer goods, and retailing.

The United States is currently the sixth largest investor in Ukraine, down from its position as the largest source of FDI in the late 1990s. U.S. investment has encompassed a number of sectors, ranging from agriculture to consumer goods to financial services. However, as investment in Ukraine began to take off in 2003, U.S. investment grew less rapidly than did a number of other countries', including Cyprus's (Figure 2.9). To some extent, this was the result of European banks showing greater interest in Ukraine's banking sector. But U.S. investors were also put off by the difficulties encountered in investing in Ukraine. Given alternative destinations for their investment dollars, they have chosen countries with larger markets (such as China, India, and Russia) or countries with more congenial investment climates (such as the Central European states or countries in East Asia).

Figure 2.9
Foreign Direct Investment in Ukraine, by Country of Origin, 2001–2006

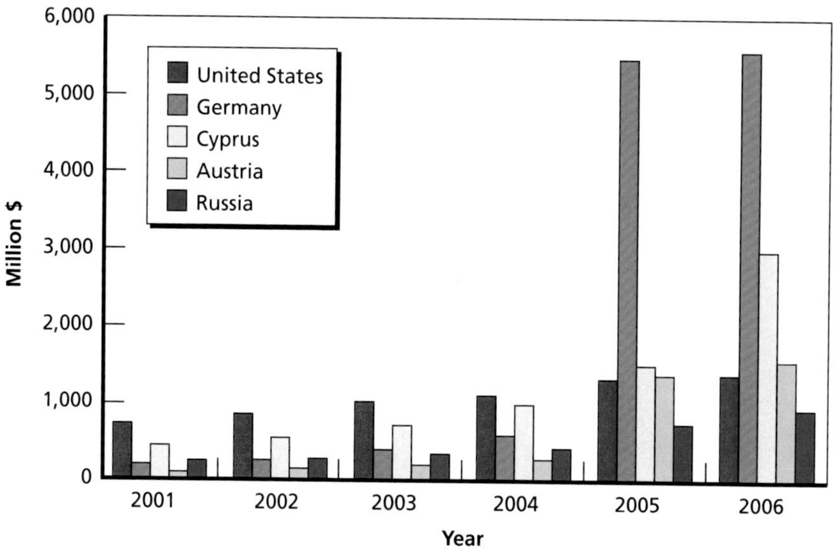

SOURCE: State Statistics Committee of Ukraine, "National Accounts," 2001–2006.
RAND *MG673-2.9*

CHAPTER THREE

Barriers to Trade and Foreign Direct Investment in Ukraine

Ukraine is beginning to tap its great potential for economic development, but it remains a frustrating country in which to trade or invest. The list of problems facing those that want to trade or invest in Ukraine is long: The original Blue Ribbon Commission Report ran 92 pages, and the European Business Association has written 154 pages of detailed recommendations to address the myriad problems it found.[1] Sadly, few of these recommendations have been adopted. According to our interviewees, major obstacles to trading or investing include those described in this chapter.

Corruption

All of our interviewees complained about the barriers to trade and investment posed by corruption. Grand corruption involves high-level officials who have discretionary authority over government policy, the sale of government assets, and large government contracts. Petty corruption involves lower-level officials who make decisions about enforcing (or not enforcing) regulations. Ukraine suffers from all of these varieties. Although Ukrainians are not alone in enduring corruption, Ukraine scores poorly compared to most other countries. On Transparency International's 2006 Corruption Perceptions Index, Ukraine

[1] Blue Ribbon Commission for Ukraine, 2005; European Business Association, 2006.

scored 99th of 163 countries, putting it firmly in the bottom half of the group.[2] Algeria, Burkina Faso, Serbia, and Romania—none of which is noted for clean government—all scored better. Russia, however, scored worse, coming in at 121.

Foreign businesses complain most vociferously about Ukrainian regulatory and legal hurdles designed to elicit bribes. As in most countries afflicted by corruption, Ukrainian government employees, in hopes of eliciting bribes, deliberately design licensing and registration procedures to be so complex that they credibly threaten to halt or slow exporting or importing operations or a foreign investment. As a consequence, the permits and licenses required to set up and open a business are difficult and expensive to obtain. Complying with all the demands from the bureaucracy, many of which are contradictory, adds considerably to the time and expense of opening a business. One interviewee noted that U.S. businessmen who visit the region for the first time to investigate business opportunities never return to Ukraine. First-time potential U.S. investors are so appalled by the demands for bribes and the regulatory and legal hurdles to trading or setting up a business that they look for opportunities elsewhere, frequently in Central Europe. Ukraine's advantages in labor and other operating costs are not great enough to compensate for the aggravation and cost of trying to work through the government bureaucracy.

Rigged privatizations are another major impediment to foreign investment. Sadly, corrupt privatization procedures have caused Ukrainians to consistently lose out as assets are sold for substantially less than their fair market value. Several international steel companies spent considerable time and effort in 2004 bidding for Krivoryzhstal, Ukraine's largest steel complex. When last-minute adjustments in the terms of reference resulted in Ukrainian investors becoming the only ones qualified to bid, foreign bidders were disgusted. When Krivoryzhstal was reprivatized in 2005, a number of the original bidders decided not to bid again. Although the reprivatization generated six times the proceeds of the original sale, Ukraine received fewer bids than it had during the first round.

---

[2] Transparency International, 2006.

Ukraine also suffers from corrupt practices in government contracting. According to our interviewees, foreign exporters and investors frequently choose not to participate in bids because they know that a Ukrainian company has already wrapped up the contract. Terms in requests for proposals are often poorly defined, the criteria by which bids are judged are often broad, and the procedures by which awards are made are opaque. Under these conditions, potentially competitive bidders choose not to bid, generally leaving the bidding to companies that are more expensive and less qualified.

Another problem is that Ukraine's judicial system is corrupt. The legal code is littered with contradictory provisions, making it possible for a company to pick and choose the laws under which it disputes a contract or other type of agreement. Precedent is not recognized, so a judge does not have to rule in accordance with previous rulings. And because it is extremely difficult to remove a judge, crooked judges operate with impunity.

Barriers to Trade

Ukraine has made substantial progress in reducing barriers to trade since 2004, especially by the reduction and consolidation of tariff rates that took place in 2005. However, a number of severe impediments remain, as discussed next.

Ukraine Is Not Yet a Member of the World Trade Organization

Despite support from all major political parties, Ukraine has still not joined the WTO. The advantages of WTO membership are many. First and foremost, membership protects Ukrainian exporters from unwarranted retaliation by trading partners that are also members—that is, all of Ukraine's major trading partners except Russia, which is on the verge of becoming a WTO member itself. WTO sets clear rules for when trading partners may adopt protectionist measures and operates a system for adjudicating disputes. Currently, whenever disputes erupt, Ukraine tends to be at the mercy of its larger trading partners. These countries have applied quotas, countervailing duties, and other protectionist measures against key Ukrainian exports such as steel pipe and bulk chemicals. As long as it remains outside the WTO, Ukraine has no formal means of recourse against these measures.

Businesses lack the surety that Ukraine's membership in WTO would provide. Because Ukraine's government is not bound by WTO's rules, it has been able to adopt protectionist regulations without public comment or restraint. Exporters and importers have been seriously damaged by unexpected regulations that affect their trade with Ukraine (such as the imposition of an embargo on grain exports in 2006); yet they have no forum in which to seek to repeal or change these regulations.

Difficulties in Obtaining Refunds for Value-Added Tax

In our view, the most severe impediment to exports from Ukraine is the corruption embedded in the system that provides rebates to exporters for the VAT they pay on inputs. As in other countries that levy VAT, exports from Ukraine are exempt. Exporters pay VAT on goods and services used to produce their items for export, and that VAT is then to be refunded by the Ukrainian government. But the government consistently delays payment or challenges the veracity of the exporters' claims. Since the standard VAT rate is 20 percent, VAT payments for inputs are often substantial; so failure or delay in reimbursing VAT payments imposes a severe penalty on exporters, discouraging exports. The effect on low-margin exports, such as grain, clothing, and labor-intensive manufactured items, is especially pernicious, since failure to refund VAT spells the difference between profit and loss. One reason why Ukrainian exports are so heavily concentrated in just a few commodities is that anyone considering exporting a different product must consider unrefunded VAT payments as a major potential source of unprofitability. For example, exports of automotive components, a major export item in Central Europe, have been slow to take off in Ukraine because nonrecovered VAT payments on materials and parts used to make the components would make this export unprofitable.

Government employees encourage companies seeking VAT refunds to hire local law or consulting firms that charge a "fee" of 25 to 30 percent of the refund to secure reimbursement. If the designated firms are hired and paid, all requested VAT refunds are reimbursed promptly. Western multinationals operate under codes of conduct and laws in their country of origin that rule out payments to obtain VAT refunds. Although most have been able to use political and legal pressures to induce the tax authorities to eventually reimburse them for VAT payments, they experience lengthy delays. Obtaining a refund for a foreign firm can take three to 18 months. Smaller companies that refuse to pay bribes receive no refunds at all. Tax authorities compound these problems by attempting to hold Western multinationals accountable for the activities of their suppliers. Some of the companies from which Western multinationals purchase inputs pocket the portion of the purchase price listed as VAT rather than hand it over to tax authorities. In response, the tax authorities choose not to tighten their own procedures but, instead, to attempt to get multinationals to compel their suppliers to obey the law by demanding that multinationals extensively document their requests for reimbursements. In some instances, the Ukrainian government has refused to provide reimbursements to multinationals whose suppliers have failed to pay VAT.

The sums involved in VAT refunds are enormous. In spring 2007, roughly 4 billion hryvnia ($785 million) in VAT refunds was overdue—that is, this amount had not been refunded within the state-mandated 60 days. The kickback schemes associated with obtaining these refunds provide large sums for patronage. Adding to the problem is the fact that tax authorities make refunds to companies falsely claiming exports, partly because the authorities are incapable of catching scam artists and at times because government employees receive bribes for processing fraudulent requests for refunds. Because of these refunds for fake exports, VAT generates little net revenue for the Ukrainian government.

Certification and Standards

Ukraine's complex, corrupt system of certifying imports imposes the greatest barrier to importers. Accepted international practice recognizes products certified by accredited bodies in partner states with internationally recognized accreditation procedures as acceptable in the importing country. In Ukraine, products subject to mandatory certification—which make up a very long list—have to be recertified. These procedures add substantial additional expense to importing and delay the introduction of new products. In a number of instances, these added costs keep manufacturers from exporting their products to Ukraine.

In the EU and the United States, manufacturers are permitted to select agencies that conduct conformity assessments from an accredited list. In Ukraine, the government designates the agencies that are to certify products, even though some of these agencies are private businesses with ties to government officials. These links between certification agencies and government regulators foster corruption and contribute to maintaining the current expensive and unnecessary system.

Ukraine's procedures for certifying compliance with Ukrainian standards for food, agricultural products, and pharmaceuticals are particularly onerous. In the case of food, despite laws to the contrary, importers are often compelled to obtain certificates from the State Department for Veterinary Medicine and the Ministry of Health. Certification is an expensive and lengthy process. In the case of perishable items, the time involved in this process can make importing prohibitive—the items can rot before certification is completed. Inspection agencies may insist on inspecting the processing facilities in which the product originated in hopes of a free trip to Europe or the United States—only to look at facilities already certified by an EU member state or the U.S. government. Meat and meat products, particularly poultry (a major U.S. export to Ukraine), face the highest barriers. Even though the law says only one agency should be responsible, three agencies claim responsibility for approving imports of meat: the State Department for Veterinary Medicine in the Ministry of Agriculture, the Sanitary Epidemiological Center in the Ministry of Health, and the State Center of Metrology Standardization and Certification. All three agencies charge for evaluating and certifying imports, and all three have kickback schemes with official nongovernment organizations that charge for inspections and certification. For example, one restaurant wholesaler that imported a single container of fish had to have it inspected by all three agencies, at a cost of $40 per inspection per type, which made the venture unprofitable.

Government bureaucracies use delaying and other tactics, many of which are illegal, to maintain complicated certification procedures. For example, after a new law on phyto and sanitary regulations was passed in March 2006, the bureaucracy delayed issuing new regulations until December 2006. While the new regulations were unavailable, the customs authorities operated under the old regulations, which they could more easily manipulate to halt imports unless they were paid bribes.

Embargoes

Nothing has served to undermine Ukraine's reputation as a responsible trading partner more than the embargoes imposed on grain exports in 2006 and 2007. Although the embargoes were explained as originating from a concern about shortages of milling wheat, the government later expanded the embargoes to include feed grains, belying the official explanation. Commercial interests tied to the government hoped to benefit from procuring export quotas that they could then sell to legitimate grain exporters, pocketing a large profit. Outside observers and foreign investors concur that the embargoes were illegal under WTO rules for imposing export restrictions. Under those rules, embargoes or export quotas may only be imposed if the country is suffering from a "critical shortage."[3] Ukraine was not facing a critical shortage: It had adequate supplies of milling wheat and no shortages at all of feed grains when it imposed the embargoes.

The embargoes inflicted losses of more than $200 million on grain exporters and farmers, and they will have a lasting, depressing effect on farm incomes.[4] Faced with what is viewed as an unpredictable, capricious government, grain exporters are reluctant to purchase grain in advance. They will be willing to purchase it only if it is sold at an appreciable discount to world market prices, enough of a discount to compensate for the high risk involved in trading grain in Ukraine.

---

3 Office of the United States Trade Representative, 2007, p. 6.

4 Office of the United States Trade Representative, 2007, p. 6.

Export Taxes

Ukraine currently imposes export taxes on scrap metal, sunflower seeds, live cattle, sheep, hides, and skins. These taxes fall on many of Ukraine's poorest citizens and benefit some of its richest. In the case of sunflower seeds, Ukrainian farmers must either smuggle their crop out through Moldova or pay a 16 percent export tax, which pushes down domestic prices. Because farmers earn only what remains after paying for fertilizers, machinery, fuel, and all the other needs of farming, the export tax reduces farm incomes by far more than the 16 percent, probably by as much as a third. The Ukrainian government argues that the taxes serve to encourage further processing of these products in Ukraine. The government neglects to ask whether this processing would take place in any event. It also neglects to ask why some of the poorest Ukrainians—cattle and sheep farmers, sunflower growers, and scrap metal collectors—should be subsidizing some of Ukraine's most profitable industries—steel mills and sunflower-oil processing facilities—which do not pay export taxes.

Barriers to Foreign Direct Investment

Complicated Regulatory and Legal Environment

The biggest barrier to FDI in Ukraine is the regulatory and legal environment. Foreign investors face complicated, lengthy procedures to register and open a business. Then, once the business is open, investors are subject to frequent tax audits and inspections from health, safety, and other agencies. Government employees do these audits and inspections frequently in order to better coerce businesses into providing bribes, threatening those that do not pay with additional audits and inspections.

Ukrainian government employees exercise wide latitude in interpreting regulations and laws, frequently flouting the letter and spirit of the law. They often use this liberty to impede business activities. Many of the individuals we interviewed stated that Ukraine's bureaucracy is even more difficult than Russia's, despite Russia's poorer ranking in the Transparency International Index.

Proposals for new laws can come from different sources in Ukraine—the Council of Ministers, the President's office, individual deputies—so Ukraine's legal environment is chaotic. Moreover, proposed laws can be altered by any of these actors at any point during the legislative process. Because there is no central institution responsible for ensuring that proposed laws are consistent with current legislation, Ukraine's laws are replete with internal contradictions. In consequence, individuals and businesses can choose the laws under which they wish to operate, and government employees can choose the laws they want to apply.

Procedures to appeal regulatory decisions are cumbersome, slow, and unreliable. In many instances, companies have to seek redress in the courts because administrative appeal processes do not exist or are biased against the appellant. Court procedures are lengthy, stretching into months and sometimes years. Judges are arbitrary; many are corrupt. Because decisions in one court are not treated as precedents in another, parties to a dispute are able to seek and select judges that are likely to be more amenable to their position. Moreover, because precedence is not binding, judges have wide discretion in deciding a case and thus are better able to solicit bribes than are their counterparts in other judicial systems. Court decisions often go to the party willing to pay the largest bribe. The lack of predictability of Ukrainian court decisions, particularly regarding contract enforcement, remains a significant concern for foreign (and domestic) businesses in Ukraine.

Availability of Land and Premises

Difficulty in obtaining land and proper premises is one of the greatest hurdles facing potential investors in Ukraine. Potential investors are unable to build distribution centers and factories because most large open areas are classified as agricultural land, and agricultural land cannot be bought or sold. This ban prevents businesses from expanding and providing jobs in poor, rural areas. Retailers complain that municipal governments control most good commercial sites. Municipal governments sell or lease these sites to favored individuals with whom they have close ties or in exchange for bribes or shares in the new development. Manufacturers have difficulty acquiring sites close to major transportation arteries or with access to railroads because municipal officials have earmarked these for their own friends. Problems in obtaining titles, construction permits, and operating permits add to costs and complexity. Foreign investors hope that if the ban on the sale of agricultural land is lifted on January 1, 2008, as promised, satisfactory sites will become available. However, the date for ending the ban has been repeatedly postponed. And even if agricultural land may be bought, it will still have to be rezoned for commercial or industrial use—no easy task in Ukraine.

Like many economic policies in Ukraine, the ban on the sale of agricultural land has inflicted heavy financial costs on Ukraine's poorest citizens. For elderly farming households, land is often their only asset. These individuals, as they reach retirement age, would like to sell their land and use the proceeds to improve their homes, move to cities to be closer to their grown children, or purchase better-quality food or needed medicines. The prohibition on the sale of agricultural land deprives them of their most valuable asset, consigning many of Ukraine's elderly to continued poverty. The inability to sell land retards development of a mortgage market, as well, making it harder for families of modest means to purchase a home.

The ban on the sale of agricultural land also penalizes individuals who choose to retain and work their farms in that their land cannot be used as a source of credit. Agricultural yields remain low in Ukraine because farmers lack the credit needed to purchase the seeds, fertilizer, and herbicides that could increase their output. If the ban is repealed, land can become a source of collateral, and farmers will be able to borrow to improve their operations.

The costs of the difficulties in acquiring land and building premises are felt in slower growth and expansion of foreign operations. Difficulties in acquiring enough acceptable sites for stores have slowed the entry of a number of major foreign retailers. Some (for example, Ikea) need to open a minimum number of stores before it becomes economic to set up distribution centers. Restaurants chains (for example, McDonald's) like to source products from within the country in which they operate but cannot afford to set up local supply operations until volume exceeds a critical level. Because of the problems these companies have had in obtaining satisfactory sites, they have delayed sourcing from Ukrainian suppliers.

Ukraine also suffers from a dearth of high-quality hotels, particularly in Kyiv. Because the Kyiv city government has dragged its collective feet in providing permits and sites for new hotels, only a handful of new high-quality hotels have been opened in Kyiv since independence. In contrast, most major cities in Russia and Central Europe now boast several high-quality hotels. Shortages of high-quality hotel rooms have excluded Kyiv from much of the global convention trade, hindered the development of tourism, and discouraged businessmen and potential investors from traveling to Ukraine. After a stay in a hotel in Kyiv, one prominent visitor decreed that any future trips would be day trips only. He would not sleep in a hotel in Kyiv again.

Inconsistencies in Commercial Law

On January 1, 2004, a new Commercial (or Economic) Code came into force in Ukraine, many provisions of which are better designed for the Soviet era than for a modern market economy. A number of this code's provisions contradict provisions in Ukraine's more market-oriented, Civil Code. Moreover, a number of the provisions constrain the freedom of companies to make normal commercial decisions, violating freedoms stipulated in Ukraine's constitution and contradicting other Ukrainian laws. As a consequence, businesses find that some activities mandated by one code violate provisions of the other.

Some Ukrainian businesses exploit these legal discrepancies to select those laws they find preferable for their current operations. If disputes arise, they choose courts that favor their choice of law or judges that are willing to be bribed to do so.

Deficiencies in Laws on Joint Stock Companies

Because of deficiencies in the laws pertaining to joint stock companies, shareholders lack key rights of ownership. Majority shareholders can use the legal system and a friendly court to issue new shares and steal assets. In some instances, minority shareholders ("raiders") have used the legal system to steal control of a company away from the majority shareholders. Among other issues, current procedures for calling shareholders' meetings may be abused to deprive other shareholders of their rights. For example, shareholders have met and then issued new shares, which they promptly acquired, diluting the value of shares held by other investors. The law also fails to recognize the rights of minority shareholders to sell their shares at a fair price if one shareholder purchases a dominant share, or the rights of a dominant shareholder to acquire all shares above a certain ownership threshold.

The absence of adequate laws protecting shareholders' rights has distorted Ukraine's capital markets. Larger firms prefer to list on foreign stock exchanges because their shares are valued more highly when they are traded in countries (such as the United Kingdom) whose legal systems clearly define shareholders' rights and provide clear legal recourse for shareholders who believe their rights have been violated. As a result, Ukraine's major private companies are absent from its stock markets. Companies that are too small to list abroad avoid local stock markets because of concerns about maintaining control. Instead of turning to capital markets, these companies rely on bank credit, much of which is short term. These companies thus are often highly leveraged and remain undercapitalized. Their financial structures are less stable than they would be if Ukrainian stock markets functioned properly.

Privatization

In contrast to the governments of Central Europe, Ukrainian governments have not used privatization extensively to attract foreign capital and business expertise. Except for a very few transparent sales of major assets, privatization has usually resulted in formerly state-owned enterprises being acquired by Ukrainian businessmen or foreign companies controlled by Ukrainians. In most instances, Ukrainian businessmen have effectively excluded foreign investors by usurping the privatization process, although Russian investors have succeeded in making a few acquisitions. Foreign investors do not participate in tenders because the outcome is likely to be decided on the basis of bribes or political connections. As a consequence, foreign investors are confined to either setting up a totally new or "green field" operation or purchasing a company from its new owners after it has been privatized.

Following the Orange Revolution, the government headed by Yuriy Yekhanurov successfully conducted one open, transparent resale of a major company, Krivoryzhstal. Our interviewees stated that under the Yanukovych government, privatization procedures have reverted to what they were under former President Leonid Kuchma. The recent privatization of a locomotive plant is a case in point: It sold for less than half of its likely fair market value to a Russian bidder who submitted the only two bids—one phony, one real.

Current privatization proposals will not attract foreign investors. They involve selling stakes of 10 to 15 percent through initial public offerings (IPOs); the state would hold onto three-quarters or more of the companies' shares. They offer foreign investors no avenue through which to bring to bear their financial, marketing, and management skills. These proposed privatizations are thus highly unlikely to attract the interest of Western investors.

Energy

Foreign investors find Ukraine's energy sector exceedingly hard to penetrate. Current laws and policies, ostensibly designed to enable foreigners to invest, effectively discourage most. For example, Ukraine has passed laws permitting companies to bid for tracts on which to explore and produce petroleum or natural gas. The agreements are for such a short time (five years) that oil majors are reluctant to bid. Companies that have bid have become entangled in long, contentious disputes over terms and conditions. The Ukrainian government does not make bidding easy. Instead of including geological data in tender documents to be sold to interested parties, the government expects bidders to develop their own data. As a result of these impediments to investment, Ukraine's natural gas production remains at 20 billion cubic meters per year, little changed from the 1990s, despite the view of most energy analysts that Ukraine—once a center of Soviet natural gas production—is capable of producing 30 to 40 billion cubic meters per year.

Ukrainian regulators have proved problematic for companies that have invested in Ukraine's energy sector. Regulators are often capricious. Some of their decisions have been in violation of the law or based on extraordinarily narrow interpretations of permissible costs. One rate board refused to cover the costs of new trucks needed to maintain the distribution system. Regulators have refused applications for rate increases because their requests for bribes were not met.

To this point, foreign investors have had no trouble getting adequate supplies of natural gas or electric power at competitive prices. However, because rate boards are reluctant to approve increases in electricity and natural gas prices, electric power and gas distribution companies have been unable to invest enough to maintain their networks. Ukrainian businesses, domestic and foreign, may suffer from service outages in the years ahead. As Russia increases its prices for natural gas, energy will be less competitively priced. Ukraine's highly differentiated system of tariffs, whereby industrial consumers pay the brunt of costs and households are subsidized, will exacerbate this problem. The system of tariffs is likely to result in sharp increases in energy costs for businesses as prices for imported natural gas continue to rise.

CHAPTER FOUR

Recommendations for Improving the Climate for Trade and Foreign Direct Investment in Ukraine

Despite its recent rapid rates of economic growth and its rich endowments of land and people, Ukraine remains a difficult place in which to trade and invest. There are numerous impediments to trade and investment, and many of them are deep seated and not easily removed. In this chapter, we offer several recommendations whose adoption would rectify the most egregious barriers to trade and investment in Ukraine. We have attempted to make these recommended policy changes as concrete and easy to implement as possible. All of them should lead to improvements for Ukrainian businesses and citizens, as well as their foreign counterparts; and these improvements should make it possible for the Ukrainian government to build political constituencies to support these changes.

Reducing Corruption

1. Reduce opportunities for government employees to manipulate the regulatory system to solicit bribes.

The primary source of petty corruption in Ukraine consists of demands from government employees for bribes in exchange for expediting requests for permits or refraining from additional inspections. The Ukrainian government should reduce opportunities for government employees to manipulate the regulatory system to solicit bribes in the following ways:

- Set up a network of regional boards to which businesses and citizens can appeal administrative decisions. These boards should be composed of civil servants, businessmen, and citizens, and should be obligated to respond to complaints within ten working days. They should have the authority to stay decisions taken by lower-level civil servants until those decisions are reviewed by higher-level administrators or administrative courts. They should have the duty to facilitate appeals to higher-level administrators or administrative courts, and they should be able to protest delaying tactics or improper decisions to higher levels. All meetings of these boards should be open to the public.
- Give Inspector Generals the authority to immediately put government employees facing credible accusations of soliciting bribes on administrative leave and to then quickly bring cases to court for resolution. Both government employees and companies engaged in bribery should be punished severely.
- Hold supervisors responsible for the behavior of their employees. Supervisors should be reprimanded or even dismissed if corrupt practices are widespread in their departments.

Such steps would send an immediate signal to both government employees and the citizenry that the current tolerance of petty corruption has ended. Given that Ukrainian citizens loath the current tolerance of corruption, this policy change should be very popular.

Fostering Trade

2. Join the WTO.

Our interviewees universally agreed that joining the WTO is the most important near-term step that the Ukrainian government can take to spur trade. The Verkovna Rada has passed the final legislative changes needed to conform to its past agreements with the WTO working group. The government should now ensure that all remaining hurdles are surmounted. If bilateral negotiations fail to resolve all issues with current WTO members that threaten to block Ukraine's entry, the

Ukrainian government should turn to the secretariat of the WTO, the U.S. government, or the European Commission for assistance in resolving remaining issues.

The value of WTO membership lies as much in reducing barriers to imports within Ukraine—which will enhance access to products and improve the competitive environment internally—as it does in reducing barriers to Ukrainian exports in foreign markets. To fully enjoy the benefits of trade, the Ukrainian government will need to fully implement its commitments to the WTO. Ukraine's foreign trade partners will undoubtedly point out areas in which Ukraine fails to fulfill its agreements, but the Ukrainian government must maintain an inter-ministerial working group with enough clout to prevent regulations and laws that violate Ukraine's agreements with the WTO from being introduced and to overturn any that are adopted. *For this reason, we recommend that the Ukrainian government give the Department on Cooperation with the WTO full authority to ensure that Ukrainian legislation and regulations remain in compliance with the WTO.*

3. Begin negotiating a free trade agreement with the EU.

Once Ukraine becomes a member of the WTO, the current Ukrainian negotiating team should immediately turn to negotiations with the EU for a free trade agreement. Such an agreement would do much to break down barriers to trade stemming from differences in standards, to improve the competitiveness of Ukrainian firms, and to facilitate visas for Ukrainians visiting EU member states. It would also position Ukraine for potential membership in the EU, which would be a welcome step for the majority of Ukrainians who, according to the polls, favor Ukraine's ultimate entry into the EU.

4. Set up a transparent, prompt system for reimbursing VAT to exporters.

The Ukrainian government should promptly reimburse exporters for VAT payments and should ensure that requests are processed within 60 days, as currently stipulated in Ukrainian law. Supervisors should be penalized if this time limit is not observed. Monthly reports on VAT rebates by region and VAT payments made by Ukraine's 100 largest companies should be made available on the Internet and in published form. A working group composed of government and business representatives should identify all areas in which differences over definitions of costs exist, and the Ukrainian government should ensure that legislative and regulatory changes to resolve these differences are made promptly. Improved VAT reimbursement will be followed by a surge in lower-margin exports that will result in more jobs and increased output, and will facilitate a shift toward a more diversified set of exports.

The Ukrainian government should not use cash flow problems as an excuse to delay reimbursement or substitute other financial instruments for cash in repaying exporters. If the Ukrainian Ministry of Finance faces cash flow problems, the government should issue bonds large enough to assure that cash reserves are adequate. The tax authorities should also improve their inspection and audit procedures in order to crack down on companies that falsify export orders so that they can make bogus requests for VAT refunds.

5. Immediately accept EU standards and certification procedures. Ukraine should immediately accept all products that conform to EU standards—once certified by the EU, a product should need no further certification in Ukraine—and should eventually adopt EU standards and certification procedures. Companies should be able to voluntarily certify their products. This change will yield instant benefits for Ukrainian consumers and businesses. The increased competition from imports will result in lower prices and a wider variety of goods. Easier access to imports will help smaller Ukrainian companies expand production and become more competitive because key inputs will be more readily available and business transactions will take place more quickly.

In the case of products subject to phyto and sanitary regulations, importers should be subject to the jurisdiction of only one agency. In other words, if a product of this type is certified by one Ukrainian agency, no other Ukrainian agency should be able to block its import. If Ukrainian agencies disagree over jurisdiction, importers should be free to import a product certified by one agency until the jurisdictional dispute is resolved. In the case of mandatory certification, importers should be able to choose among accredited Ukrainian certification institutes.

6. Immediately eliminate all remaining embargoes.

The Ukrainian government should immediately eliminate all remaining embargoes on grains. It should pass legislation conforming to WTO practices that strictly defines when export quotas on agricultural products may be imposed and how they are to be allocated. This change will enable grain traders to offer higher prices, which will increase farmers' incomes. It will also increase the value of agricultural land and improve farm-sector operations because banks and traders will be willing to offer credit.

7. Accelerate the phaseout of all export taxes.

The Ukrainian government should phase out all export taxes over the course of the next three years, cutting the existing tax rates by one-third in each successive year. This change will boost the incomes of the sunflower and livestock farmers and the scrap metal collectors, some of Ukraine's poorest people.

8. Phase out special economic zones.

In 2005, the Ukrainian government eliminated all special economic zones, which many companies were using to avoid VAT and import duties on products sold within Ukraine. Three of these zones were reinstated in 2006. The Ukrainian government should not reinstate any more of these zones and should notify investors in the reinstated zones that the zones will be phased out over a fixed period. The government should refrain from providing preferential treatment to companies, Ukrainian or foreign. All companies in Ukraine should compete on a level playing field. By curbing special benefits for favored companies, the government will reduce corruption and prevent tax revenues from slipping away through special schemes involving these zones.

Attracting Foreign Direct Investment

9. Set legal limits on the ability of government employees to impede the establishment of businesses in Ukraine.

The Ukrainian government should

- Set fixed deadlines for action on permits. Permits for which action is not taken by the specified deadline should be granted automatically.
- Set a yearly limit on the number of inspections to which a business is subject.
- Ensure that initiatives for one-stop registration of businesses and issuance of permits are operating by January 1, 2008.

10. Ensure that the decision to repeal the ban on agricultural land sales goes into effect on January 1, 2008.

The Ukrainian government should ensure that the ban on sales of agricultural land is repealed on January 1, 2008. In the interim, the government should ensure that all the needed elements for land markets are in place. In particular, it should ensure that the process of titling and registering agricultural land is completed and that the titling and registration offices are coordinating their work. Additionally, the government should ensure that procedures for rezoning have been streamlined so that agricultural land can be used for construction of commercial establishments, housing, and other buildings. Of all government policies since the privatization of land, this one will provide the single largest boost to the wealth of Ukrainians living in villages. It should be highly popular in rural areas.

11. Abolish the Commercial Code and appoint a task force to rectify remaining inconsistencies in Ukraine's commercial laws.

The Ukrainian government should immediately repeal the Commercial Code. Simultaneously, it should appoint a task force composed of representatives from the judiciary, government agencies, the legal profession, businesses, and consumer groups to review the Civil Code and other laws affecting Ukrainian businesses that are contradictory, poorly written, or lacking. The task force should provide draft legislation or regulations to fix the problems identified. Additionally, the Cabinet should appoint a small team of senior government officials to spearhead efforts to make the necessary legislative changes. This team should provide the Cabinet with monthly reports on progress and estimates of when the requisite legislative changes will be made.

12. Push the joint stock company law through the Rada.

The Cabinet sent a first draft of a joint stock company law to the last Rada. The Rada should pass this law, with any modifications suggested by the business and financial communities to ensure its conformance to EU laws, within the first 100 days of its first sitting.

13. Accelerate privatization through transparent trade sales and IPOs.

The government should replace its current privatization strategy with a new one geared toward rapid, transparent sale of almost all commercial assets that it still owns. The government should draw up a revised list of companies to be privatized and an accelerated time schedule for privatization. It should also establish clear procedures for issuing tenders for trade sales, permit all interested parties to bid, and publish the terms of all bids and the winning bid. The highest bid should win. For larger companies, such as Ukrtelecom and Ukrnaftohaz, the Ukrainian government should examine the use of IPOs for the sale of sizable portions of these companies. A renewed commitment to privatization should yield substantial revenues for the government that can be used to make the pension system solvent and to invest in public infrastructure.

The Ukrainian government cannot afford to ignore the theft of government property. If government assets were obtained fraudulently during past privatizations, the government has a duty to prosecute those involved and seek restitution. However, as with all crimes, fraudulent sales of government assets should be subject to time limits; and the value of the asset should be taken into account when determining the extent of government efforts to seek restitution. The Ukrainian government should establish clear legal procedures for investigating fraud in the sale of government assets. It should also set a firm period within which a fraud can be prosecuted and stipulate that only higher-value privatizations—for example, those pertaining to assets of over 50 million hryvnia ($10 million) in value—be prosecuted.

14. Seek FDI in the energy sector.

Energy is an area in which Ukraine could greatly benefit from FDI. Ukraine is one of the world's most wasteful consumers of energy. All of its energy imports come through one country, Russia; and its state-owned mines and oil and gas producers are inefficient and lack modern technologies. Further, the country is facing substantial price increases for its imports of a major fuel, natural gas.

The Ukrainian government should adopt standard production sharing agreements of ten to 20 years, rather than the current five years, to encourage investment in domestic energy production. The government should also increase the wholesale prices of Ukrainian natural gas so that they match those of imported gas. Currently, Ukraine pays far more for gas imports from Russia and Central Asia than it pays to its own gas producers. Domestic producers should receive the same prices received by companies that export gas to Ukraine.

The Ukrainian government should permit foreign investors to participate in the construction and ownership of new gas and oil transit pipelines. The government could maintain a "golden share" in such companies so that it can veto any moves to consolidate a majority of shares into the hands of one company or group of companies. Ownership should not be a major problem as long as the Ukrainian government continues to regulate transit charges or levies taxes on oil and gas passing through the pipelines. Although Russian companies might take a large stake in a new transit pipeline, it is in Ukraine's long-term strategic interests to remain the foremost transit country for Russian and Central Asian energy. Otherwise, new pipelines, such as the proposed Nord Stream and South Stream, may circumvent Ukraine, thereby lessening its energy security.

Setting Priorities and Sequencing

Not everything can be changed at once. The Ukrainian government should adopt a two-pronged strategy to remove the worst of the impediments to trade and FDI. The first prong should focus on making a few highly visible policy changes that promise results within 100 days from the time the government announces initiatives to remove the impediments. The second prong should set in motion changes in Ukraine's institutions that will reduce the corruption and complexities currently hampering trade and FDI. These second-prong changes will take longer to bear fruit but are crucial to improving the environment for trade and investment in Ukraine. They will have to be accompanied by systems created specifically to ensure that the needed changes are being enacted and to make course corrections if and when any changes are seen as being derailed or circumvented.

Immediate Priorities, to Be Implemented Within 100 Days

- Reduce opportunities for government employees to manipulate the regulatory system to solicit bribes.
- Complete regulatory and legal changes needed to join the WTO.
- Set up a transparent, prompt system for reimbursing VAT to exporters.
- Accept EU standards and certification procedures.
- Eliminate all remaining embargoes.
- Ensure that the repeal of the ban on agricultural land sales goes into effect on January 1, 2008.
- Abolish the Economic Code and appoint a task force to rectify remaining inconsistencies in Ukraine's commercial laws.
- Push the joint stock company law through the Rada.

Longer-Term Priorities

- Negotiate a free trade agreement with the EU.
- Phase out all export taxes.

- Phase out special economic zones.
- Set legal limits on the ability of government employees to impede the establishment of businesses in Ukraine.
- Accelerate privatization through transparent trade sales and IPOs.
- Seek FDI in the energy sector.

References

Blue Ribbon Commission for Ukraine, *Proposals to the President—The New Wave of Reform: On Track to Succeed*, United Nations Development Programme, Kyiv, Ukraine, 2005. As of August 9, 2007:
http://www.un.org.ua/brc/brci/index.php?page=report

European Business Association, *Barriers to Investment in Ukraine*, 2001, 2004, 2005, and May 2006 editions, Kyiv, Ukraine. As of August 9, 2007:
http://www.eba.com.ua/analytical/barriers.html

Eurostat, "National Accounts: Gross Domestic Product," 2006. As of August 9, 2007:
http://epp.eurostat.ec.europa.eu/portal/page?_pageid=1996,45323734&_dad=portal&_schema=PORTAL&screen=welcomeref&open=/&product=EUROIND_NA&depth=2

International Monetary Fund, *International Financial Statistics*, Washington, D.C., May 2007. As of August 9, 2007:
http://www.imfstatistics.org/imf/

Office of the United States Trade Representative, *2007 National Trade Estimate Report on Foreign Trade Barriers*, Ukraine section, Washington, D.C., April 2007. As of August 9, 2007:
http://www.ustr.gov/Document_Library/Reports_Publications/2007/2007_NTE_Report/Section_Index.html

PlanEcon, "Ukraine," *PlanEcon Quarterly Report*, Volume Vol. XXI, No. 5, February 6, 2006.

State Statistics Committee of Ukraine, "National Accounts," various years. As of August 9, 2007 (English ["ENG"] can be selected at top right of page):
http://www.ukrstat.gov.ua/

Transparency International, *Corruptions Perception Index 2006*, Berlin, Germany, 2006. As of August 9, 2007:
http://www.transparency.org/policy_research/surveys_indices/global/cpi

World Bank, *Ukraine: Poverty Assessment—Poverty and Inequality in a Growing Economy*, Report No. 34631-UA, Washington, D.C., December 2005. As of August 10, 2007:
http://web.worldbank.org/WBSITE/EXTERNAL/COUNTRIES/ECAEXT/EXTECAREGTOPPOVRE0,,contentMDK:20613610~pagePK:34004173~piPK:34003707~theSitePK:904723,00.html